Practical Guide to GraphQL

Practical Guide

A. De Quattro

Practical Guide

1.Introduction

Introduction to GraphQL

GraphQL is a query language for APIs developed by Facebook in 2012 and made public in 2015. It is both a query language for APIs and a runtime for executing those queries on your existing data. It offers a more flexible and powerful alternative to traditional REST services, thanks to its ability to allow clients to request exactly the data they need—no more, no less. This technology has quickly gained popularity and adoption across the software development world, especially in modern web and mobile applications.

What is GraphQL

GraphQL, short for "Graph Query Language," is a query language for APIs that enables clients to request only the data they need. Instead of having a traditional REST API with multiple endpoints, each returning a predefined set of data, GraphQL centralizes data requests into a single endpoint. With a GraphQL query, you can request exactly the information you need, structuring it in a predefined format. This approach offers greater efficiency and flexibility compared to conventional REST APIs.

Core Principles

The core of GraphQL is the schema definition, which represents data types and relationships between them. Each schema is defined using a Schema Definition Language (SDL) that describes the possible operations a client can perform, including data types, queries, mutations, and subscriptions.

The three main operations in GraphQL are:

- **Query:** Used to read data. GraphQL queries allow you to specify exactly which fields you want to retrieve, thereby reducing the amount of data transferred and optimizing the efficiency of requests.

- **Mutations:** Used to modify data. Mutations can create, update, or delete data on the server. Similarly, the client can specify which fields they want to receive in the response.

- **Subscription:** Used to establish a continuous connection and receive real-time updates. This is particularly useful for applications that require instant feedback, such as chat applications or real-time notifications.

Data Types in GraphQL

GraphQL supports a wide range of data types, which are primarily divided into scalar types and object types:

- **Scalar Types:** These are the basic data types and include `Int`, `Float`, `String`, `Boolean`, and `ID`. They are used to represent single values such as integers, floating-point numbers, text strings, boolean values, and unique identifiers.

- **Object Types:** These represent complex entities that can have multiple fields and relationships with other object types. An object type might be, for example, a `User` with fields such as `name`, `email`, and `age`.

GraphQL also allows for defining custom types, enums, and interfaces to better model application-specific data.

Query Execution

When a client sends a query to a GraphQL server, the server parses the query based on the defined schema. The server then executes the query on the underlying data and returns a response structured exactly as specified in the query. This reduces the overhead of unwanted data and simplifies the management of responses on the client side.

History and Development of GraphQL

GraphQL was initially developed by Facebook in 2012 as a necessity to improve the performance of their mobile applications. At that time, Facebook faced several challenges with traditional API infrastructure. The growing complexity of mobile user interfaces required a more efficient way to fetch specific data from the server without loading unnecessary data.

The Need for a Solution

Before the development of GraphQL, Facebook used REST APIs to serve data to their applications. However, with increasing feature requests and a higher dependence on mobile devices, the REST approach was showing significant limitations. REST APIs were prone to problems such as over-fetching and under-fetching. With over-fetching, clients received more information than needed, slowing down mobile app performance, while under-fetching required multiple API calls to obtain all necessary data, increasing latency and complexity.

The Birth of GraphQL

In 2012, a small team of engineers at Facebook began developing GraphQL as an internal solution to these issues. GraphQL was designed to be a strongly-typed query language that allowed clients to specify exactly what data they wanted, thus reducing overhead and latency.

GraphQL was initially implemented within Facebook's mobile application, and the results were immediate. Developers were able to build features faster, with a more responsive user interface and fewer performance issues.

The Release of GraphQL

After three years of internal use and refinement, Facebook decided to release GraphQL as an open-source project in 2015. The release was accompanied by the publication of documentation and tools needed to start using GraphQL. Since then, the technology has gained popularity, with an increasing number of companies and developers adopting it in their applications.

Evolution and Community

Since its release, GraphQL has seen rapid growth and adoption in the developer community. The GraphQL ecosystem has been enriched by numerous tools, libraries, and server-side implementations in various programming languages, including JavaScript, Python, Ruby, Go, and others. The community has also contributed to improving the specification and developing new features, such as subscriptions and enhancements in authorization and security management.

In 2018, the GraphQL Foundation was formed under the Linux Foundation to oversee and promote the continued development of GraphQL. This organization is responsible for managing the progress of the GraphQL specification and supporting the development of related tools and community efforts.

Advantages of GraphQL over REST

GraphQL offers several advantages over traditional REST APIs, making it an attractive choice for many developers and companies. These advantages include:

1. **Flexible Requests and Data Precision**

One of the primary benefits of GraphQL is the ability to request exactly the data needed without receiving unnecessary or incomplete data. In a REST API, each endpoint returns a fixed set of data, which means you might receive more data than necessary (over-fetching) or have to make multiple requests to get all desired information (under-fetching).

With GraphQL, the client can specify exactly which fields to include in the response. For example, if you only need a user's name and email, you can request only those fields, avoiding the receipt of other unnecessary data such as address or phone number. This approach reduces the amount of data transferred and makes applications more efficient.

2. **A Single Endpoint for All Operations**

Traditional REST APIs require creating and maintaining a significant number of endpoints to support all necessary operations and data combinations. This approach can become complex and difficult to manage as the application grows.

GraphQL, on the other hand, uses a single endpoint through which all operations are performed. This greatly simplifies API management and reduces the number of HTTP requests needed. Developers only need to manage and document one endpoint, with the client specifying the exact structure of the desired response.

3. **Static Typing and Self-Documentation**

One of the strengths of GraphQL is its strongly-typed nature. Each data type and relationship in the system is defined in the GraphQL schema, allowing clients to know exactly which fields are available and what type of data to expect. This not only improves data security and integrity but also makes it easier to develop tools for automatic analysis and validation.

Moreover, due to its typing, GraphQL offers almost automatic documentation. Tools like GraphiQL and GraphQL Playground allow developers to explore the API and write queries interactively, with automatic suggestions based on the schema. This reduces the time and effort required to create and maintain manual API documentation.

4. **Handling Data Relationships**

Another limitation of REST APIs is handling relationships between different types of data. In REST, obtaining related data often requires multiple API calls, which need to be orchestrated by the client, increasing complexity and latency.

In GraphQL, data relationships are an integral part of the schema. You can navigate between related data types within a single query. For example, in one request, you can get a list of users along with their posts and comments on each post, all in one operation. This reduces the number of round trips required and simplifies interaction with the API.

5. **Effective Updates and Modifications with Mutations**

Mutations in GraphQL allow for updating, creating, or deleting data with the same flexibility and precision as queries. This means you can specify exactly which data you want to receive in response after making a modification, avoiding the need for additional requests to get updated data.

Additionally, due to the structured nature of mutations, it's easier to manage write operations and ensure that the data is updated correctly on the client without needing extra requests to synchronize the application's state.

6. **Subscriptions for Real-Time Updates**

One of the most innovative aspects of GraphQL is its native support for subscriptions. Subscriptions allow receiving real-time updates when data changes on the server. This is especially useful for applications requiring continuous feedback, such as chat applications, notification systems, or interactive dashboards.

Subscriptions eliminate the need for custom solutions or continuous polling to get updates, providing an elegant and scalable mechanism for keeping data synchronized between server and client.

7. **Modern Ecosystem and Tooling**

The GraphQL ecosystem has rapidly expanded, with a vast array of tools and libraries that simplify the adoption and integration of GraphQL into existing applications. There are GraphQL servers available for most major programming languages, including JavaScript, Python, Ruby, PHP, Go, and others.

Tools like Apollo, Relay, and Hasura provide ready-to-use solutions for integrating GraphQL with databases, managing caching, implementing authorization, and optimizing query performance. These tools make GraphQL not only a powerful technology but also accessible and easy to integrate into a wide range of environments and tech stacks.

8. **Support for Field Deprecation**

In GraphQL, managing the evolution of an API and deprecating fields without breaking backward compatibility is straightforward. Developers can mark fields as `@deprecated`, providing a reason and suggesting alternative usage. This helps maintain API stability over time, allowing for evolution and adoption of new practices without disrupting the functionality of existing applications.

GraphQL represents a significant step forward compared to

 traditional REST APIs, offering greater flexibility, efficiency, and ease of use for developers. With its ability to handle complex requests through a single endpoint, reduce data overhead, and support real-time updates, GraphQL has become a crucial tool in the modern development landscape. Its growing adoption and expanding ecosystem indicate that GraphQL will continue to play a key role in the future of APIs and web and mobile architectures.

2.Fundamental Concepts of GraphQL

GraphQL is a powerful query language that enables clients to communicate with servers in a flexible and precise manner. It was designed to address many of the limitations of traditional REST APIs, such as data over-fetching and multiple calls to retrieve related information. To fully understand GraphQL, it's essential to know the fundamental concepts at its core: schema, data types, queries, mutations, and subscriptions. Additionally, understanding how GraphQL handles data fetching, server responses, and its typing and validation system is crucial.

GraphQL Schema

The schema is the heart of any GraphQL implementation. It defines the data types, the available operations (queries, mutations, and subscriptions), and the relationships between them. The schema acts as a contract between the client and the server, describing what requests are possible and what data can be returned.

Data Types

In GraphQL, data types represent the structure of the available data. They can be divided into several main categories:

1. **Scalar Types**: Scalar types represent primitive values and are the fundamental building blocks for more complex types. The predefined scalar types in GraphQL are:

   - `Int`: A 32-bit integer.

   - `Float`: A double-precision floating-point number.

   - `String`: A sequence of text characters.

   - `Boolean`: A boolean value, which can be `true` or `false`.

   - `ID`: A unique identifier, often used for unique references.

2. **Object Types**: Object types are complex structures that can contain multiple fields of various types, including other object types. For example:

```graphql
type User {
  id: ID!
  name: String!
  age: Int
  email: String!
  posts: [Post]
}

type Post {
  id: ID!
  title: String!
  content: String
  author: User!
```

```
}
```

In this example, `User` and `Post` are object types. The `posts` field within `User` is an array of `Post` objects, showing a one-to-many relationship between `User` and `Post`.

3. **Enumeration (enum) Types**: An enum type represents a limited set of possible values. It is useful for defining fields that can only take on a restricted number of values. For example:

```graphql
enum Role {
  ADMIN
  USER
  GUEST
}
```

```graphql
type User {

  id: ID!

  name: String!

  role: Role!

}
```
```

In this case, `Role` is an enum that defines three possible values: `ADMIN`, `USER`, and `GUEST`.


4. **Interfaces and Unions**: Interfaces define a set of fields that an object type must implement. Unions allow combining multiple types, enabling a field to be one type or another. For example:


```graphql
interface SearchResult {
```
```

```graphql
  id: ID!
}


type User implements SearchResult {
  id: ID!
  name: String!
}


type Post implements SearchResult {
  id: ID!
  title: String!
}


union Search = User | Post


type Query {
  search(query: String!): [SearchResult]
}
```

```
```

Here, `SearchResult` is an interface implemented by `User` and `Post`, while `Search` is a union that can return either a `User` or a `Post`.

5. **Input Types**: Input types are similar to object types but are used exclusively as inputs for mutations. For example:

```graphql
input CreateUserInput {
  name: String!
  email: String!
  age: Int
}

type Mutation {
  createUser(input: CreateUserInput): User
```

```
}
```
```

In this example, `CreateUserInput` is an input type used to provide the data necessary to create a new user.

#### Queries

Queries are the central element of GraphQL for data retrieval. A query is similar to a GET request in a REST API but offers greater flexibility and precision. The client can specify exactly which fields it wants to retrieve, and the server will return only those fields.

Example of a query:

```graphql
query GetUser {
```
```

```
user(id: "1") {

  id

  name

  email

  posts {

    title

    content

  }

 }

}
```
```

In this query, the client requests a specific
user with ID "1" and specifies the `id`,
`name`, `email`, and an array of associated
posts with the fields `title` and `content`. The
server will return only the requested data,
minimizing unnecessary data overhead.


#### Mutations
```

Mutations are used in GraphQL to modify data, such as creating, updating, or deleting entities. Unlike queries, mutations can have side effects on the server state.

Example of a mutation:

```graphql
mutation CreateUser {
  createUser(input: { name: "Alice", email: "alice@example.com", age: 30 }) {
    id
    name
    email
  }
}
```

This mutation creates a new user with the fields `name`, `email`, and `age`, and returns the `id`, `name`, and `email` fields of the newly created user. Mutations in GraphQL are always specific and allow determining the structure of the response, just like queries.

Subscriptions

Subscriptions in GraphQL allow clients to receive real-time updates when certain events occur on the server. This is particularly useful for applications that require a continuous flow of data, such as chat applications, notifications, or real-time dashboards.

Example of a subscription:

```graphql
subscription OnNewPost {
  newPost {
```

```
    id

    title

    content

    author {

      name

    }

  }

}

```
```

This subscription notifies the client whenever a new post is created. The new post's data, including `id`, `title`, `content`, and the author's information, will be sent to the client as soon as the event occurs.

How GraphQL Works

GraphQL operates through a well-defined workflow that includes client data requests,
```

server-side processing of those requests, data typing and validation, and finally, returning a structured response. Understanding this process is key to fully leveraging GraphQL's potential.

Data Fetching

When a client sends a request to a GraphQL server, it is sent in the form of a query, mutation, or subscription. Each request specifies exactly what data the client wants to retrieve or what operations it wants to perform. The server receives this request and analyzes it based on the defined schema.

1. **Parsing and Validation**: The server begins by examining the query to ensure it is syntactically correct and that all requested operations conform to the schema. This validation process ensures that the client is requesting existing fields and that the requested data types are correct.

2. **Query Execution**: Once the query has been validated, the server proceeds with execution. This involves interacting with various data layers (databases, external services, etc.) to retrieve the requested information. GraphQL allows defining resolvers, which are functions responsible for obtaining the data for each requested field.

Example of a resolver:

```javascript
const resolvers = {
  Query: {
    user: (parent, args, context, info) => {
      return fetchUserFromDatabase(args.id);
    },
  },
  User: {
    posts: (parent, args, context, info) => {
```

```
      return fetchPostsByUserId(parent.id);
    },
  },
};
```

In this example, `user` is a resolver for the `user` field of the query, which retrieves the user from the database using the provided ID. The `posts` resolver retrieves the posts associated with the user.

3. **Query Optimization**: Another advantage of GraphQL is the ability to optimize queries through batching and caching. For example, GraphQL can group multiple similar requests to reduce the number of database calls, thereby improving the overall performance of the API.

Server Response

Once the server has processed the query and retrieved the necessary data, it constructs a JSON response. The structure of the response matches the structure of the query sent, making it easy for the client to process the returned data.

Example of a response:

```json
{
  "data": {
    "user": {
      "id": "1",
      "name": "Alice",
      "email": "alice@example.com",
      "posts": [
        {
          "title": "GraphQL for Beginners",
          "content": "GraphQL is a query
```

language for APIs..."

```
        },
        {
            "title": "Advanced GraphQL",
            "content": "Let's dive deeper into
GraphQL..."
        }
    ]
    }
  }
}
```

In this example, the server returned the data exactly in the form requested by the query. This approach eliminates the need for complex parsing or client-side transformations, as the data is already organized according to the client's needs.

Typing and Validation

Typing is one of the key aspects of GraphQL. Every field in the GraphQL schema is associated with a type, and every query or mutation must conform to these type definitions. Typing allows GraphQL to offer several advantages:

1. **Security and Reliability**: Thanks to strong typing, GraphQL can ensure that every request made by the client is valid according to the schema. This helps prevent common errors, such as requesting a field that doesn't exist or passing an incorrect data type.

2. **Automatic Documentation**: Since the schema defines all data types and their relationships, it is possible to automatically generate detailed and accurate documentation for the API. Tools like GraphiQL and GraphQL Playground use typing to provide suggestions and autocomplete when writing queries, enhancing the development

experience.

3. **Validation**: During the validation process, GraphQL ensures that the query conforms to

the schema. This includes checking that all data types are correct, that there are no missing fields, and that mutations respect the defined constraints. If a query fails validation, GraphQL returns a descriptive error, making debugging easier.

Example of a validation error:

```json
{
  "errors": [
    {
      "message": "Cannot query field \"age\" on type \"User\".",
```

```
"locations": [

  {

    "line": 2,

    "column": 5

  }

  ]

}

]

}
```
```

This error message indicates that the `age` field does not exist on the `User` type and specifies exactly where the error is located in the query, making it easier to correct.

GraphQL is a powerful technology that revolutionizes how applications interact with APIs. Through its strict and typed schema, flexible and precise operations like queries,
```

mutations, and subscriptions, and its robust validation mechanism, GraphQL offers unprecedented control over data.
Understanding these fundamental concepts is essential for fully leveraging GraphQL's capabilities, improving efficiency, security, and the developer experience in building and maintaining modern applications.

3.Setting Up a GraphQL Server

Creating a GraphQL server requires a deep understanding of backend technology, project structure, and the configuration of key tools like Apollo Server and GraphQL Yoga. This guide will explore each stage of the process in detail, including defining the GraphQL schema, which is fundamental for modeling the API's data and operations.

Choosing the Backend Technology

Before setting up a GraphQL server, it's essential to select the backend technology that best suits the project's needs. GraphQL is programming language-agnostic, meaning it can be implemented in various backend environments such as Node.js, Python, Ruby, Java, and others.

1. Node.js with JavaScript/TypeScript

Node.js is a popular choice for implementing

GraphQL servers due to its speed and extensive library ecosystem. JavaScript and TypeScript (a typed version of JavaScript) are commonly used with Node.js to build GraphQL servers. Frameworks like Express.js can be easily integrated with GraphQL through libraries like Apollo Server or GraphQL Yoga.

2. Python with Django/Flask

For those who prefer Python, Django and Flask are two popular frameworks. Django can be integrated with Graphene, a library that supports the development of GraphQL servers in Python. Flask, being a micro-framework, offers greater flexibility to integrate GraphQL through libraries like `flask-graphql`.

3. Ruby on Rails

Ruby on Rails, a widely-used framework, can use `graphql-ruby`, a gem that provides the necessary tools to create a GraphQL server. Rails is known for its convention over configuration, which can simplify integration with GraphQL.

4. Java with Spring Boot

In Java, Spring Boot is one of the most used frameworks for building backend applications. The `graphql-java` library provides support for creating robust GraphQL servers in Java, integrating well with Spring Boot's modular architecture.

5. Go (Golang)

Go, with its emphasis on performance and simplicity, is another excellent option. Libraries like `graphql-go` allow for the development of efficient GraphQL servers in Go, offering a lightweight and fast programming experience.

GraphQL Project Structure

The structure of a GraphQL project varies depending on team preferences and the application's complexity, but there are some common best practices that can help organize the code efficiently and scalably.

1. `src/` Folder

The `src/` folder contains all the application's source code. Within `src/`, it's useful to further divide the code into modules or features. A possible organization could be:

- `src/schema/`: Contains the GraphQL schema, divided into files that define various types, queries, mutations, and subscriptions.

- `src/resolvers/`: Contains resolvers, which are functions that implement the business logic to respond to queries and mutations.

- `src/models/`: Data models that represent entities in the database, especially useful if using an ORM (Object-Relational Mapping).

- `src/context/`: Defines the context passed to the resolvers, often used for handling authentication, authorization, and data access.

2. Configuration Files

- `index.js` or `app.js`: The application's entry point, where the server is initialized and GraphQL is configured.

- `.env`: File for environment variables, useful for configuring sensitive parameters like API keys or database credentials.

3. Tests

- `tests/`: This folder should contain the application's tests. Testing a GraphQL API can include unit tests for resolvers and integration tests for queries and mutations.

Configuring Apollo Server

Apollo Server is one of the most widely used libraries for creating GraphQL servers in Node.js. It offers a range of advanced features, including caching, error handling, and integration with various databases and authentication tools.

1. Installation

To start with Apollo Server, you need to install the main dependencies:

```bash
npm install apollo-server graphql
```

2. Basic Configuration

The following code shows how to set up a basic Apollo Server:

```javascript
const { ApolloServer, gql } = require('apollo-server');

// Schema definition
```

```
const typeDefs = gql`
  type Query {
    hello: String
  }
`;


// Resolvers
const resolvers = {
  Query: {
    hello: () => 'Hello, world!',
  },
};


// Creating the server
const server = new ApolloServer({ typeDefs,
resolvers });


// Starting the server
```

```
server.listen().then(({ url }) => {

  console.log(`Server ready at ${url}`);

});
```
```

In this example, a simple schema is defined with a `hello` query that returns a string. The server is started and listens on a default port, usually `http://localhost:4000`.


**3. Database Integration**


Apollo Server can be easily integrated with a database to retrieve and manipulate data. For example, if using MongoDB, you can configure a resolver to interact with the database:


```javascript
const { MongoClient } = require('mongodb');
```
```

```
// Connect to the MongoDB database
const client = new
MongoClient('mongodb://localhost:27017');

client.connect();


const resolvers = {
  Query: {
    users: async () => {
      const db = client.db('mydatabase');

      return await
db.collection('users').find().toArray();

    },

  },

};

```
```

This resolver retrieves a list of users from the
MongoDB database and returns them as the
```

result of the `users` query.

Configuring GraphQL Yoga

GraphQL Yoga is another popular GraphQL server for Node.js, based on Express. It is known for its simplicity and ease of use, making it an excellent choice for those seeking a quick and flexible solution.

1. Installation

To start with GraphQL Yoga, you need to install the dependencies:

```bash
npm install @graphql-yoga/node graphql
```

2. Basic Configuration

A simple server with GraphQL Yoga can be configured as follows:

```javascript
const { createServer } = require('@graphql-yoga/node');

// Schema definition
const typeDefs = `
  type Query {
    greeting: String
  }
`;

// Resolvers
const resolvers = {
  Query: {
    greeting: () => 'Hello from Yoga!',
```

```
  },
};


// Creating the server
const server = createServer({
  schema: {
    typeDefs,
    resolvers,
  },
});


// Starting the server
server.start(() => {
  console.log('Server is running on
http://localhost:4000');
});
```
```
```

In this example, the server responds to a `greeting` query with a simple message. Yoga is known for its support for GraphQL Subscriptions, which allows for implementing real-time features easily.

3. Middleware and Extensions

GraphQL Yoga supports middleware and extensions that can be used to add features such as authentication, logging, or error handling. For example, to add a logging middleware:

```javascript
const loggingMiddleware = async (resolve, root, args, context, info) => {

  console.log('Request received');

  const result = await resolve(root, args, context, info);

  console.log('Request processed');
```

```javascript
    return result;

};


const server = createServer({

  schema: {

    typeDefs,

    resolvers,

  },

  middlewares: [loggingMiddleware],

});
```
```

#### Example Implementation of a GraphQL Server

Now let's combine all the elements into an example implementation of a more complex GraphQL server. This example includes an Apollo Server configuration with a MongoDB database.
```

1. Project Structure

```plaintext
/my-graphql-server
├── src
│   ├── schema
│   │   ├── typeDefs.js
│   │   └── resolvers.js
│   ├── models
│   │   └── user.js
│   ├── context.js
│   └── index.js
├── .env
└── package.json
```

2. Schema and Resolvers

In `src/schema/typeDefs.js`, define the schema:

```javascript
const { gql } = require('apollo-server');

const typeDefs = gql`
  type User {
    id: ID!
    name: String!
    email: String!
  }

  type Query {
    users: [User]
    user(id: ID!): User
  }
```

```
  type Mutation {

    createUser(name: String!, email: String!):
User

  }
`;



module.exports = typeDefs;
```

In `src/schema/resolvers.js`, implement the resolvers:

```javascript
const User = require('../models/user');


const resolvers = {
  Query: {
    users: async () => await User.find(),
```

```
    user: async (_, { id }) => await
User.findById(id),

  },

  Mutation: {

    createUser: async (_, { name, email }) => {

      const user = new User({ name, email });

      await user.save();

      return user;

    },

  },

};


module.exports = resolvers;
```
```

**3. User Model**


In `src/models/user.js`, define the user model
using Mongoose for MongoDB:
```

```javascript
const mongoose = require('mongoose');

const userSchema = new mongoose.Schema({
  name: {
    type: String,
    required: true,
  },
  email: {
    type: String,
    required: true,
    unique: true,
  },
});

const User = mongoose.model('User', userSchema);
```

```javascript
module.exports = User;
```

4. Context and Server Configuration

In `src/context.js`, configure the context:

```javascript
module.exports = ({ req }) => {

  // For example, get the token from the header
for authentication

  const token = req.headers.authorization || ";

  return { token };

};
```

Finally, in `src/index.js`, configure and start
the server:

```javascript
const { ApolloServer } = require('apollo-server');

const mongoose =

 require('mongoose');
const typeDefs = require('./schema/typeDefs');
const resolvers = require('./schema/resolvers');
const context = require('./context');


mongoose.connect(process.env.MONGO_URI, {
  useNewUrlParser: true,
  useUnifiedTopology: true,
});


const server = new ApolloServer({
  typeDefs,
```

```
  resolvers,

  context,

});


server.listen().then(({ url }) => {

  console.log(`Server ready at ${url}`);

});
```

5. Running the Server

To start the server, run the following commands:

```bash
npm install

npm start
```

Ensure that the MongoDB URI is set in the `.env` file:

```env
MONGO_URI=mongodb://localhost:27017/mydatabase
```

This comprehensive example shows how to set up a GraphQL server with Apollo Server, connect it to a MongoDB database, and define the schema and resolvers to handle queries and mutations.

Testing and Deploying

Once the server is set up, it's crucial to thoroughly test all aspects of the API, including edge cases, error handling, and performance under load. GraphQL servers can be tested using tools like Jest for unit tests and Apollo's own testing utilities.

For deployment, consider using platforms like Heroku, AWS, or Vercel, which offer support for Node.js applications. These platforms provide tools to handle scaling, monitoring, and managing environment variables securely.

By following this guide, you should have a solid foundation for setting up a GraphQL server that is organized, scalable, and ready for production.

4.Writing and Using Queries in GraphQL

GraphQL is a powerful and flexible query language designed for interacting with APIs. Unlike REST, GraphQL allows clients to specify exactly which data they want to request and how it should be structured. In this section, we'll explore in detail how to write and use queries in GraphQL, from basic syntax to more advanced concepts like aliases, fragments, and variables.

Query Syntax

The syntax of GraphQL queries is concise and readable. Queries are composed of several key components:

- **Operation Type**: `query`, `mutation`, or `subscription`. If not specified, a query is assumed.

- **Operation Name** (optional): An optional name that can be used to identify the query, particularly useful in debugging or complex operations.

- **Fields**: The fields are what you request from the API. Each field corresponds to a piece of data available on the server.

- **Arguments** (optional): Some fields can accept arguments to filter or configure the response.

Here is an example of a simple GraphQL query:

```graphql
{
  user(id: "1") {
    id
    name
    email
  }
}
```

```
```

In this query, the client requests the information of a specific user (`user`), including the `id`, `name`, and `email` fields.

Basic Queries

Basic queries in GraphQL allow you to request simple data from the server. A typical example of a basic query is requesting a list of objects or a single object with a subset of fields.

Example of a basic query to get a list of users:

```graphql
{
  users {
    id
```

```
    name

    email

  }

}

```
```

This query returns a list of users, each with the `id`, `name`, and `email` fields. The response might look like this:

```json
{

  "data": {

    "users": [

      {

        "id": "1",

        "name": "Alice",

        "email": "alice@example.com"

      },
```
```

```
      {
        "id": "2",
        "name": "Bob",
        "email": "bob@example.com"
      }
    ]
  }
}
```

Nested Queries

One of the strengths of GraphQL is the ability
to perform nested queries, which means
requesting related data in a single operation.
For example, you might request a user and, at
the same time, all their posts.

Example of a nested query:

```graphql
{
  user(id: "1") {
    id
    name
    posts {
      title
      content
    }
  }
}
```

This query requests the details of a specific user and their posts (`posts`), each with a `title` and `content`. The response will be structured so that the requested data is nested:

```json
{
  "data": {
    "user": {
      "id": "1",
      "name": "Alice",
      "posts": [
        {
          "title": "GraphQL Basics",
          "content": "An introduction to GraphQL..."
        },
        {
          "title": "Advanced GraphQL",
          "content": "Deep dive into GraphQL features..."
        }
      ]
    }
```

```
  }

 }

 ```
```

Aliases and Fragments

Aliases

Aliases allow you to rename fields in the
response, which is useful when requesting
multiple instances of the same field with
different arguments.

Example of using aliases:

```graphql
{

  firstUser: user(id: "1") {

    name

  }
```
```

```
  secondUser: user(id: "2") {

    name

   }

 }

```
```

The response will be:

```json
{

  "data": {

    "firstUser": {

      "name": "Alice"

    },

    "secondUser": {

      "name": "Bob"

    }

  }
```
```

```
}
```
```

**Fragments**

Fragments are useful for reusing groups of fields in different parts of the query. They help avoid code duplication and keep queries more organized.

Example of using fragments:

```graphql
{
  user(id: "1") {
    ...userDetails
  }
  users {
    ...userDetails
  }
```
```

```
}


fragment userDetails on User {

  id

  name

  email

}
```
```

In this example, the `userDetails` fragment is defined once and then reused in multiple locations within the query.


#### Variables in Queries


Variables in GraphQL allow queries to be dynamic and reusable. Instead of hardcoding fixed values in the query, you can pass variables that are substituted at runtime.
```

Example of using variables:

```graphql
query getUser($id: ID!) {
  user(id: $id) {
    id
    name
    email
  }
}
```

This query requires an `$id` parameter, which will be used to retrieve the user data. Variables are passed separately, typically in a JSON object:

```json
{
```

```
    "id": "1"

}
```

This allows the same query to be executed with different values to obtain different results.

Practical Examples of Queries

1. Retrieve a list of products with related details:

```graphql
{
  products {
    id
    name
    price
```

```
    category {

      name

      }

    }

  }

```

The response will include a list of products with the name of the category they belong to:

```json
{

  "data": {

    "products": [

      {

        "id": "101",

        "name": "Laptop",

        "price": 1500,
```

```
        "category": {
          "name": "Electronics"
        }
      },
      {
        "id": "102",
        "name": "Coffee Maker",
        "price": 80,
        "category": {
          "name": "Home Appliances"
        }
      }
    ]
  }
}
```

**2. Using aliases and fragments to customize

the response:**

```graphql
{
  cheapProduct: product(price: "50") {
    ...productDetails
  }
  expensiveProduct: product(price: "1500") {
    ...productDetails
  }
}

fragment productDetails on Product {
  id
  name
  price
}
```

This example renames the results for cheap and expensive products and reuses the `productDetails` fragment.

Handling Mutations

Mutations in GraphQL are equivalent to create, update, and delete operations in REST. While queries are used to retrieve data, mutations are used to modify it.

Concept of Mutation

A mutation is a GraphQL request that changes the state of data on the server. It is similar to a query, but instead of requesting data, it performs an action that can modify existing data or create new data. Mutations can also return data, allowing clients to immediately update the user interface with the new data.

Mutation Syntax

The syntax of mutations is similar to that of queries, but with some key differences:

- **Operation Type**: Begins with the keyword `mutation`.

- **Operation Name**: Optional, as in queries.

- **Fields**: Fields represent the operations to be performed. Each field can have arguments that specify the data to create or modify.

Example of a mutation to create a new user:

```graphql
```

```
mutation {

  createUser(name: "Alice", email:
"alice@example.com") {

    id

    name

    email

  }

}
```
```

This mutation creates a new user with the
provided name and email, and returns the `id`,
`name`, and `email` fields of the created user.


#### Mutation Responses


One of GraphQL's key features is that
mutations can return data just like queries.
This allows you to immediately get the results
of the performed operation without having to
```

make a separate query.

Example of a response for the `createUser` mutation:

```json
{
  "data": {
    "createUser": {
      "id": "1",
      "name": "Alice",
      "email": "alice@example.com"
    }
  }
}
```

In this way, the client immediately knows which user was created and can update the user interface accordingly.

Practical Examples of Mutations

1. Create a new product:

```graphql
mutation {
  createProduct(name: "Smartphone", price: 799, categoryId: "2") {
    id
    name
    price
  }
}
```

This mutation creates a new product with the name "Smartphone," a price of 799, and associates it with a specific category. The response might be:

```json
{
  "data": {
    "createProduct": {
      "id": "103",
      "name": "Smartphone",
      "price": 799
    }
  }
}
```

2. Update the details of an existing user:

```graphql
```

```
mutation {

  updateUser(id: "1", email:
"newalice@example.com") {

    id

    name

    email

  }

}
```
```

This mutation updates the email of the user
with `id` 1. The response will return the
updated details:

```json
{

  "data": {

    "updateUser": {

      "id": "1",
```
```

```
      "name": "Alice",

      "email": "newalice@example.com"

    }

   }

}
```

3. Delete a product:

```graphql
mutation {
  deleteProduct(id: "103") {
    id
    name
  }
}
```

This mutation deletes a specific product. The response will confirm the deletion:

```json
{
  "data": {
    "deleteProduct": {
      "id": "103",
      "name": "Smartphone"
    }
  }
}
```

In these examples, we have seen how mutations in GraphQL are powerful tools for modifying data state on the server while maintaining full control over the data returned to the client.

5.Using Subscriptions in GraphQL

Subscriptions in GraphQL are among the most powerful and innovative features of the language. While queries and mutations allow you to retrieve and manipulate data, subscriptions enable clients to receive real-time updates whenever there are changes to the data. This is particularly useful in applications where the user interface needs to be constantly updated with fresh information, such as in messaging systems, financial dashboards, or online games.

What is a Subscription?

A subscription in GraphQL is a real-time connection between the client and the server, where the client subscribes to specific events and receives updates whenever these events occur. Unlike queries and mutations, which are executed once, a subscription can persist over time, sending data to the client whenever the server signals a change.

Subscriptions are often implemented using protocols like WebSocket, which allow for bidirectional and persistent communication between the server and the client.

Example of a subscription in GraphQL:

```graphql
subscription {
  messageAdded {
    id
    content
    author {
      name
    }
  }
}
```

In this example, the client subscribes to the `messageAdded` event, which is triggered every time a new message is added to the system. The server will send the client the details of the new message (`id`, `content`, and `author.name`) each time one is created.

Implementing Subscriptions

To implement subscriptions in GraphQL, you need to configure the server to support real-time connections, in addition to handling queries and mutations. Subscriptions are often integrated into GraphQL servers like Apollo Server, which provides advanced tools for managing real-time connections.

1. Configuring Apollo Server for Subscriptions

Apollo Server supports subscriptions through the use of WebSocket, which needs to be configured alongside the standard HTTP server.

Install the necessary dependencies:

```bash
npm install @apollo/server graphql-ws ws
```

These dependencies include Apollo Server, support for GraphQL WebSocket, and a WebSocket server.

Configure the server:

```javascript
const { ApolloServer } =
require('@apollo/server');

const { makeExecutableSchema } =
require('@graphql-tools/schema');
```

```javascript
const { useServer } = require('graphql-
ws/lib/use/ws');

const { WebSocketServer } = require('ws');

const http = require('http');


// Define the GraphQL schema
const typeDefs = `
  type Message {
    id: ID!
    content: String!
    author: User!
  }


  type User {
    id: ID!
    name: String!
  }
```

```
type Query {

  messages: [Message!]

}


type Mutation {

  addMessage(content: String!, authorId:
ID!): Message!

}


type Subscription {

  messageAdded: Message!

}
`;


const resolvers = {

  Query: {

  messages: () => { /*...*/ },

},
```

```
Mutation: {

  addMessage: (parent, { content, authorId },
{ pubsub }) => {

    const newMessage = { id:
Date.now().toString(), content, authorId };

    // Publish the event

    pubsub.publish('MESSAGE_ADDED',
{ messageAdded: newMessage });

    return newMessage;

  },

  },

  Subscription: {

   messageAdded: {

    subscribe: (parent, args, { pubsub }) =>
pubsub.asyncIterator(['MESSAGE_ADDED'])
,

    },

   },

  };
```

```javascript
// Create the executable schema

const schema =
makeExecutableSchema({ typeDefs, resolvers
});


// Configure the HTTP and WebSocket server

const server = http.createServer();

const wsServer = new WebSocketServer({

  server,

  path: '/graphql',

});


useServer({ schema }, wsServer);


const apolloServer = new
ApolloServer({ schema });

await apolloServer.start();


server.listen(4000, () => {
```

```
  console.log('Server ready at
http://localhost:4000/graphql');

});
```
```

In this example, we have configured Apollo
Server to support subscriptions. Subscriptions
are handled via the `WebSocketServer`, and
the HTTP server is used to handle standard
requests (queries and mutations).


**2. Defining Resolvers for Subscriptions**


Resolvers for subscriptions differ from those
for queries and mutations because they return
an `AsyncIterator`, which allows sending
multiple results over time.


Example of a subscription resolver:


```javascript
```
```

```
const resolvers = {

  Subscription: {

   messageAdded: {

    subscribe: (parent, args, { pubsub }) =>
pubsub.asyncIterator(['MESSAGE_ADDED'])
,

   },

  },

};
```

```
```

In this resolver, the `subscribe` method uses a `pubsub.asyncIterator` to listen for the `MESSAGE_ADDED` event. When the event is published, the client subscribed to the subscription receives the related data.

3. Handling WebSocket Connections from the Client

A GraphQL client, such as Apollo Client, can be configured to support subscriptions using WebSocket.

Install the dependencies on the client:

```bash
npm install @apollo/client subscriptions-transport-ws graphql-ws
```

Configure the client:

```javascript
import { ApolloClient, InMemoryCache, split, HttpLink } from '@apollo/client';

import { getMainDefinition } from '@apollo/client/utilities';

import { WebSocketLink } from '@apollo/client/link/ws';
```

```javascript
// Configure the HTTP link
const httpLink = new HttpLink({
  uri: 'http://localhost:4000/graphql',
});

// Configure the WebSocket link
const wsLink = new WebSocketLink({
  uri: `ws://localhost:4000/graphql`,
  options: {
    reconnect: true,
  },
});

// Logic to route subscriptions through WebSocket and the rest through HTTP
const splitLink = split(
  ({ query }) => {
```

```
    const definition =
getMainDefinition(query);

  return (

    definition.kind === 'OperationDefinition'
&&

    definition.operation === 'subscription'

  );

 },

 wsLink,

 httpLink

);


const client = new ApolloClient({

 link: splitLink,

 cache: new InMemoryCache(),

});
```
```

With this configuration, the client can handle
```

both HTTP requests and WebSocket subscriptions.

Practical Examples of Using Subscriptions

1. Real-Time Chat System:

A classic example of using subscriptions is a real-time chat system.

Chat Schema:

```graphql
type Message {
  id: ID!
  content: String!
  sender: User!
}
```

```
type User {
  id: ID!
  name: String!
}

type Query {
  messages: [Message!]
}

type Mutation {
  sendMessage(content: String!, senderId: ID!): Message!
}

type Subscription {
  messageReceived: Message!
}
```

```
```

Subscription Resolver:

```javascript
const resolvers = {
  Subscription: {
    messageReceived: {
      subscribe: (parent, args, { pubsub }) =>
pubsub.asyncIterator(['MESSAGE_RECEIVE
D']),
    },
  },
  Mutation: {
    sendMessage: (parent, { content,
senderId }, { pubsub }) => {
      const newMessage = { id:
Date.now().toString(), content, senderId };
      pubsub.publish('MESSAGE_RECEIVED',
{ messageReceived: newMessage });
```

```javascript
    return newMessage;
   },
  },
};
```

Client to Receive Messages:

```javascript
import { gql, useSubscription } from
'@apollo/client';

const MESSAGE_RECEIVED = gql`
 subscription {
  messageReceived {
   id
   content
   sender {
```

```
      name
      }
    }
  }
`;


function ChatComponent() {
  const { data, loading } =
  useSubscription(MESSAGE_RECEIVED);


  if (loading) return <p>Loading...</p>;
  return (
    <div>
      <p>{data.messageReceived.sender.name}:
{data.messageReceived.content}</p>
    </div>
  );
}
```

In this example, every time a new message is sent using the `sendMessage` mutation, all clients subscribed to the `messageReceived` subscription will receive the message in real time.

2. Stock Price Monitoring:

Imagine an application that monitors stock prices and updates the user whenever a stock's price changes.

Stock Price Monitoring Schema:

```graphql
type Stock {
  symbol: String!
  price: Float!
}
```

```
type Query {
  stock(symbol: String!): Stock
}

type Subscription {
  stockPriceUpdated(symbol: String!): Stock!
}
```

Subscription Resolver:

```javascript
const { PubSub } = require('apollo-server');
const pubsub = new PubSub();

const resolvers = {
  Subscription: {
    stockPriceUpdated: {
```

```
  subscribe: (parent, { symbol },
{ pubsub }) => {

    // Use asyncIterator to receive updates on
the stock price

    return
pubsub.asyncIterator(`STOCK_PRICE_UPD
ATED_${symbol}`);

    },

  },

},

Mutation: {

  updateStockPrice: (parent, { symbol,
price }, { pubsub }) => {

    // Logic to update the stock price in the
database

    const updatedStock = { symbol, price };


    // Publish the update for all subscribers


pubsub.publish(`STOCK_PRICE_UPDATED
_${symbol}`, { stockPriceUpdated:
```

```
  updatedStock });

    return updatedStock;
  },
 },
};
```

In this case, the `updateStockPrice` mutation updates the price of a stock and publishes the update using `pubsub.publish`. All clients subscribed to the `stockPriceUpdated` subscription for the specific symbol will receive the update in real time.

Client to Receive Price Updates:

```javascript
import { gql, useSubscription } from '@apollo/client';
```

```
const STOCK_PRICE_UPDATED = gql`
  subscription stockPriceUpdated($symbol: String!) {
    stockPriceUpdated(symbol: $symbol) {
      symbol
      price
    }
  }
`;


function StockPriceComponent({ symbol }) {
  const { data, loading } = useSubscription(STOCK_PRICE_UPDATED, {
    variables: { symbol },



});
```

```
if (loading) return <p>Loading...</p>;

return (

  <div>

    <p>{data.stockPriceUpdated.symbol}: $
{data.stockPriceUpdated.price}</p>

  </div>

 );

}

```
```

With this client setup, the stock price will be updated automatically whenever the server receives a new price.

Subscriptions in GraphQL open up powerful possibilities for building dynamic, real-time applications. Whether you're developing a
```

chat application, monitoring stock prices, or anything else that benefits from real-time data, GraphQL subscriptions allow you to push updates to clients efficiently and effectively. The ability to seamlessly handle both query-based and event-driven data makes GraphQL a versatile choice for modern application development.

6.Tools and Libraries for GraphQL

GraphQL is a powerful query language for APIs that has gained considerable popularity due to its flexibility and ability to optimize communications between clients and servers. To support the adoption and implementation of GraphQL, there are various tools and libraries that simplify the creation, consumption, and testing of GraphQL APIs. In this section, we will explore the main GraphQL clients, development tools, and popular libraries, and delve into how GraphQL requests work on different platforms.

GraphQL Clients

GraphQL clients are tools used to interact with GraphQL servers. They handle sending queries and mutations and receiving responses. GraphQL clients often offer advanced features like caching, state management, and integration with front-end frameworks.

1. Defining a Client in JavaScript

One of the most popular clients for JavaScript is Apollo Client, but there are also other clients like Relay and Urql. Apollo Client is well-known for its rich functionality and integration with various JavaScript frameworks like React, Angular, and Vue.

Apollo Client:

Installation:

```bash
npm install @apollo/client graphql
```

Apollo Client Configuration:

```javascript
import { ApolloClient, InMemoryCache, HttpLink } from '@apollo/client';

const client = new ApolloClient({
  link: new HttpLink({ uri: 'http://localhost:4000/graphql' }),
  cache: new InMemoryCache(),
});

export default client;
```

Usage Example with React:

```javascript
import React from 'react';
import { ApolloProvider, useQuery, gql }
```

```javascript
from '@apollo/client';

const GET_USERS = gql`
  query GetUsers {
    users {
      id
      name
      email
    }
  }
`;

function Users() {
  const { loading, error, data } =
  useQuery(GET_USERS);

  if (loading) return <p>Loading...</p>;

  if (error) return <p>Error:
{error.message}</p>;
```

```
  return (
    <ul>
      {data.users.map(user => (
        <li key={user.id}>{user.name}
({user.email})</li>
      ))}
    </ul>
  );
}


function App() {
  return (
    <ApolloProvider client={client}>
      <Users />
    </ApolloProvider>
  );
}
```

export default App;

```
```

In this example, Apollo Client is configured to interact with a GraphQL server and manages cache state and queries within a React app.

2. Clients for the Java Virtual Machine (JVM)

For the JVM, there are several libraries available to interact with GraphQL servers.

GraphQL Java Client:

Installation with Maven:

```xml
```

```
<dependency>
  <groupId>com.graphql-java-kickstart</groupId>
  <artifactId>graphql-java-client</artifactId>
  <version>11.0.0</version>
</dependency>
```

Using GraphQL Java Client:

```java
import com.graphql_java_generator.client.GraphqlClient;
import com.graphql_java_generator.client.GraphqlClientFactory;

public class GraphQLClientExample {
    public static void main(String[] args) {
```

```java
        GraphqlClient client =
GraphqlClientFactory.create("http://localhost:
4000/graphql");


        String query = "{ users { id name email }
}";

        String response = client.execute(query);


        System.out.println(response);

    }

}
```

In this example, we use `graphql-java-client` to send a query and receive a JSON response.

3. PHP Client

For PHP, a common library is `graphql-client`.

Installation with Composer:

```bash
composer require softonic/graphql-client
```

Using the PHP Client:

```php
require 'vendor/autoload.php';

use Softonic\GraphQL\Client;
use Softonic\GraphQL\Query;

$client = new Client('http://localhost:4000/graphql');
```

```php
$query = (new Query('GetUsers'))
    ->setQuery('{
      users {
        id
        name
        email
      }
    }');


$response = $client->runQuery($query);

print_r($response->getData());
```

4. Python Client

In Python, `gql` is a useful library for interacting with GraphQL servers.

Installation:

```bash
pip install gql
```

Using the Python Client:

```python
from gql import Client, gql

client =
Client(transport=RequestsHTTPTransport(url
='http://localhost:4000/graphql'))

query = gql('''
    query GetUsers {
        users {
```

```
        id

        name

        email

    }

  }
""")


result = client.execute(query)

print(result)
```

5. Android Client

For Android, you can use Apollo Android to manage GraphQL queries.

Installation:

Add to `build.gradle`:

```groovy
dependencies {
    implementation 'com.apollographql.apollo:apollo-runtime:3.0.0'
}
```

Using the Android Client:

```java
import com.apollographql.apollo.ApolloClient;

import com.apollographql.apollo.api.Response;

import okhttp3.OkHttpClient;

import okhttp3.logging.HttpLoggingInterceptor;
```

```java
public class GraphQLClientExample {

    private static final String BASE_URL =
"http://localhost:4000/graphql";


    public static void main(String[] args) {

        HttpLoggingInterceptor logging = new
HttpLoggingInterceptor();


logging.setLevel(HttpLoggingInterceptor.Lev
el.BODY);


        OkHttpClient httpClient = new
OkHttpClient.Builder()

                .addInterceptor(logging)

                .build();


        ApolloClient apolloClient =
ApolloClient.builder()

                .serverUrl(BASE_URL)
```

```
        .okHttpClient(httpClient)

        .build();


    // Use the ApolloClient instance to
execute queries and mutations

    }

}

```

Development Tools for GraphQL

Development tools help design, test, and document GraphQL APIs. Some of the most popular tools include:

1. GraphiQL

GraphiQL is a user interface for exploring and testing GraphQL APIs. It provides an interactive environment where developers can write and test queries, explore the schema, and see results in real time.

2. Apollo Studio

Apollo Studio is a suite of tools for managing GraphQL APIs, including features for documentation, performance monitoring, and schema management. It is useful for teams working with GraphQL on a large scale.

3. Insomnia

Insomnia is a REST and GraphQL client that provides a user-friendly interface for testing APIs. It supports managing GraphQL queries and mutations and includes advanced features like data and parameter management.

4. Postman

Postman, primarily known for REST APIs, has added support for GraphQL, allowing users to test and document queries and mutations directly in the app.

Popular Libraries for GraphQL

1. Apollo Client

Apollo Client is one of the most comprehensive and popular libraries for managing GraphQL requests in JavaScript clients. It offers an advanced caching system and integration with many modern frameworks.

2. Relay

Relay is a library developed by Facebook for managing GraphQL data. It is particularly suited for React applications and focuses on cache management and query prefetching to optimize performance.

3. Urql

Urql is a lightweight and flexible GraphQL client for JavaScript, designed to be easy to use and extensible. It is a good choice for applications that require a simple and customizable client.

Testing in GraphQL

Testing is crucial to ensure that GraphQL APIs work as expected and handle all requests and responses correctly.

1. Query Testing Techniques

Queries can be tested using testing tools like Jest along with specific GraphQL libraries. You can mock server responses to verify that the client handles data correctly.

Query Testing Example with Jest:

```javascript
import { ApolloClient, InMemoryCache, HttpLink } from '@apollo/client';

import { MockedProvider } from '@apollo/client/testing';

import { render, screen } from '@testing-library/react';

import Users from './Users'; // React component using Apollo Client

const mocks = [
  {
    request: {
      query: GET_USERS,
    },
```

```
    result: {
      data: {
        users: [
          { id: '1', name: 'Alice', email:
'alice@example.com' },
          { id: '2', name: 'Bob', email:
'bob@example.com' },
        ],
      },
    },
  },
];


test('renders users', async () => {
  render(
    <MockedProvider mocks={mocks}
addTypename={false}>
      <Users />
    </MockedProvider>
```

);


```
  expect(await
screen.findByText('Alice')).toBeInTheDocum
ent();

  expect(await
screen.findByText('Bob')).toBeInTheDocume
nt();

});
```
```


In this example, `MockedProvider` is used to simulate a server response and test the React component that consumes the query.


**2. Mutation Testing**


Mutation testing is similar to query testing. You can mock mutation responses and verify that the client handles state changes correctly.
```

Mutation Testing Example with Jest:

```javascript
import { ApolloClient, InMemoryCache, HttpLink } from '@apollo/client';

import { MockedProvider } from '@apollo/client/testing';

import { render, screen, fireEvent } from '@testing-library/react';

import CreateUser from './CreateUser'; // React component using Apollo Client


const mocks = [
  {
    request: {
      query: CREATE_USER,
      variables: { name: 'Charlie', email: 'charlie@example.com' },
    },
    result: {
```

```
    data: {
      createUser: {
        id: '3',
        name: 'Charlie',
        email: 'charlie@example.com',
      },
    },
   },
  },
];


test('creates a new user', async () => {
 render(
   <MockedProvider mocks={mocks} addTypename={

false}>
     <CreateUser />
```

```
      </MockedProvider>
  );


  fireEvent.click(screen.getByText('Create
User'));


  expect(await
screen.findByText('Charlie')).toBeInTheDocu
ment();
});
```
```

**3. End-to-End Testing**


End-to-end (E2E) testing tools like Cypress
can be used to test GraphQL queries and
mutations in the context of a running
application. This approach ensures that the
application behaves correctly in real-world
scenarios.
```

End-to-End Testing Example with Cypress:

```javascript
describe('User management', () => {
  it('creates a new user and displays it', () => {
    cy.visit('/users');

    cy.intercept('POST', '/graphql', (req) => {
      if (req.body.operationName ===
'CreateUser') {
        req.reply({
          data: {
            createUser: {
              id: '3',
              name: 'Charlie',
              email: 'charlie@example.com',
            },
          },
```

```
    });

  }

  });



cy.get('input[name="name"]').type('Charlie');

cy.get('input[name="email"]').type('charlie@e
xample.com');

  cy.get('button').contains('Create
User').click();


  cy.contains('Charlie');

  cy.contains('charlie@example.com');

 });

});
```

This Cypress test simulates user interaction
and verifies that the application correctly

creates and displays a new user using GraphQL.

Summary

Understanding and utilizing GraphQL clients, development tools, and libraries are essential for building efficient, scalable, and maintainable GraphQL applications. Whether you're working with JavaScript, JVM-based languages, PHP, Python, or Android, there are tools and libraries available to streamline your workflow. Testing your GraphQL APIs ensures their reliability and robustness, making them ready for production use.

7.Best Practices and Optimization in GraphQL

When working with GraphQL, it is essential to follow best practices and optimize the performance of the API to ensure it is robust, scalable, and maintainable. In this section, we will explore best practices for error handling, schema documentation, performance optimization, and the use of batching and caching. We will also examine advanced examples of GraphQL usage, such as implementation with microservices, integration with NoSQL databases, and adoption of serverless architectures.

Error Handling

Effective error handling is crucial to ensure that GraphQL APIs are reliable and that clients receive clear and useful feedback. GraphQL provides a standard format for error handling, but it is important to implement error handling correctly on both the server and client sides.

1. Server-Side Errors

In GraphQL, errors are returned in the `errors` field of the response object. Each error is represented as an object with a `message` field describing the error and, optionally, a `locations` field indicating where the error occurred in the query.

Example of Error Response:

```json
{
  "data": null,
  "errors": [
    {
      "message": "User not found",
      "locations": [
```

```
      {
        "line": 2,
        "column": 3
      }
    ],
    "path": [
      "user"
    ]
  }
 ]
}
```

2. Error Handling in Resolvers

Resolvers should handle errors appropriately
and return detailed information when
necessary. The `try-catch` construct can be
used to catch exceptions and return formatted

errors.

Example of Error Handling in Resolvers (Node.js):

```javascript
const resolvers = {
  Query: {
    user: async (parent, { id }, context) => {
      try {
        const user = await getUserById(id);
        if (!user) {
          throw new Error('User not found');
        }
        return user;
      } catch (error) {
        throw new Error(`Error fetching user: ${error.message}`);
      }
```

```
    },

   },

};

```

3. Validation Errors

Always validate incoming requests and handle validation errors with clear messages.

Example of Validation:

```javascript
const resolvers = {

  Mutation: {

    createUser: (parent, { input }) => {

      if (!input.email.includes('@')) {

        throw new Error('Invalid email address');
```

```
      }

      // Proceed with user creation

    },

  },

};
```
```

#### Schema Documentation

Good schema documentation is essential for facilitating development and API integration. GraphQL provides some built-in features for documentation, but it's also important to adopt best practices.

**1. Use Descriptions for Types and Fields**

GraphQL allows you to add descriptions to types and fields in your schema. These descriptions can be viewed through tools like
```

GraphiQL or Apollo Studio.

Example of Descriptions in Schema:

```graphql
"""
Represents a user in the system.
"""
type User {
  """
  The ID of the user.
  """
  id: ID!

  """
  The name of the user.
  """
  name: String!
```

```
"""

The email address of the user.

"""

email: String!

}
```
```

**2. Documentation Tools**

Use automated documentation tools to generate and view interactive documentation for your schema. Some popular tools include:

- **GraphiQL**: Provides an interface for exploring and testing your GraphQL schema.

- **Apollo Studio**: Offers advanced monitoring and documentation features for GraphQL APIs.

- **GraphQL Playground**: An alternative to
```

GraphiQL that offers a modern interface and many additional features.

Performance Tuning

Performance optimization is crucial to ensure that the GraphQL API responds quickly even under load. Key aspects of performance optimization include using efficient queries, tuning resolvers, and implementing caching and batching.

1. Query Optimization

Ensure that queries are optimized and do not request unnecessary data. Use monitoring tools to identify slow queries and analyze their impact on performance.

2. Resolver Optimization

Resolvers should be designed to be as efficient as possible. Avoid costly and repetitive operations within resolvers and use optimized database queries.

Example of Resolver Optimization:

```javascript
const resolvers = {
  Query: {
    user: async (parent, { id }) => {
      // Use an optimized database query
      return await db.users.findById(id);
    },
  },
};
```

3. Using Batching and Caching

Batching:

Batching allows combining multiple requests into a single call to reduce the number of round-trips between client and server. Use DataLoader for batching requests.

Example of Batching with DataLoader:

```javascript
const DataLoader = require('dataloader');

const userLoader = new DataLoader(async (keys) => {

  const users = await db.users.find({ _id: { $in: keys } });

  return keys.map(key => users.find(user => user.id === key));
});
```

```
const resolvers = {

  Query: {

    user: (parent, { id }) =>
userLoader.load(id),

  },

};
```
```

**Caching:**

Caching can reduce server load and improve query performance. Apollo Client and other GraphQL clients offer built-in caching solutions.

**Example of Caching with Apollo Client:**

```javascript
import { ApolloClient, InMemoryCache,
HttpLink } from '@apollo/client';
```
```

```
const client = new ApolloClient({

  link: new HttpLink({ uri:
'http://localhost:4000/graphql' }),

  cache: new InMemoryCache(),

});
```
```

### Advanced GraphQL Examples

GraphQL can be used in a variety of advanced scenarios to address specific challenges, such as integration with microservices, NoSQL databases, and serverless architectures.

#### Microservices with GraphQL

GraphQL can serve as an aggregation layer over microservices, facilitating integration and communication between different services.
```

Example of Microservices Aggregation:

Suppose you have two microservices: one for users and one for posts. You can use GraphQL to aggregate data from both services into a single API.

Example Schema:

```graphql
type Query {
  user(id: ID!): User
  posts(userId: ID!): [Post]
}

type User {
  id: ID!
  name: String!
```

```
  email: String!

}


type Post {

  id: ID!

  title: String!

  body: String!

  userId: ID!

}
```

Example Resolvers:

```javascript
const resolvers = {

  Query: {

    user: async (parent, { id }, context) => {

      return await
```

```
fetchUserFromUserService(id);
    },

    posts: async (parent, { userId }, context) =>
{

      return await
fetchPostsFromPostService(userId);
    },
  },
};
```
```

In this example, the `user` and `posts` resolvers fetch data from different microservices and aggregate them through a single GraphQL API.

#### GraphQL with NoSQL Databases

GraphQL can be used with NoSQL databases like MongoDB or Cassandra, providing
```

flexibility in data management.

Example with MongoDB:

Example Schema:

```graphql
type Query {
  books: [Book]
}

type Book {
    id: ID!
    title: String!
    author: String!
}
```

Example Resolvers with MongoDB:

```javascript
const { MongoClient } = require('mongodb');
const client = new MongoClient('mongodb://localhost:27017');
const db = client.db('library');

const resolvers = {
  Query: {
    books: async () => {
      return await db.collection('books').find().toArray();
    },
  },
};
```

In this example, book data is retrieved from

MongoDB and returned through a GraphQL API.

GraphQL and Serverless

Adopting a serverless architecture with GraphQL can simplify scalability and reduce operational costs.

Example with AWS Lambda and Apollo Server:

Example Schema:

```graphql
type Query {
  hello: String
}
```

AWS Lambda Configuration with Apollo Server:

```javascript
const { ApolloServer, gql } = require('apollo-server-lambda');

const typeDefs = gql`
  type Query {
    hello: String
  }
`;

const resolvers = {
  Query: {
    hello: () => 'Hello world!',
  },
};
```

```
const server = new ApolloServer({ typeDefs,
resolvers });


exports.graphqlHandler =
server.createHandler();
```
```

In this example, Apollo Server is configured to run as an AWS Lambda function, offering a scalable and serverless GraphQL API.


By following best practices for error handling, schema documentation, performance optimization, and using batching and caching, you can build scalable and reliable GraphQL APIs. Advanced examples demonstrate how GraphQL can be effectively used with microservices, NoSQL databases, and serverless architectures, providing flexible and scalable solutions for a variety of scenarios. By adhering to these best practices and leveraging optimization techniques, you can
```

ensure that your GraphQL API is performant and maintainable.

8.GraphQL Glossary

The GraphQL glossary includes the fundamental terms and concepts associated with this API technology. Understanding these terms is essential for working effectively with GraphQL and fully leveraging its capabilities.

1. **API (Application Programming Interface)**

  - **Definition**: An interface that allows different applications to communicate with each other. In GraphQL, the API is an interface that defines how clients can interact with the server to fetch or modify data.

2. **Batching**

  - **Definition**: A technique for grouping multiple requests into a single call to improve performance and reduce the number of round-trips between the client and server. GraphQL can utilize batching through tools like

DataLoader to combine data requests into a single query.

3. **Caching**

- **Definition**: A technique for temporarily storing data to reduce access times and improve performance. GraphQL uses caching to store query responses and enhance the speed of future requests.

4. **Client**

- **Definition**: An application or library that consumes the GraphQL API to request data and interact with the server. Examples include Apollo Client and Relay.

5. **Context**

- **Definition**: An object passed to resolvers that can contain shared information, such as user data, configurations, or database connections. It is used to access common data and services during the processing of a query or mutation.

6. **DataLoader**

 - **Definition**: A library that implements batching and caching to reduce the number of requests to the database or other data sources. It is used to optimize data access and improve the performance of GraphQL APIs.

7. **Documentation**

 - **Definition**: Detailed description of the types and fields available in a GraphQL schema. Documentation helps developers understand how to use the API and explore the possibilities offered by the server.

8. **Enum (Enumeration Type)**

 - **Definition**: A scalar type that represents a limited set of possible values. Used to define fixed and predefined values in a GraphQL schema.

 Example:

```graphql
enum Role {
  ADMIN
  USER
  GUEST
}
```

9. **Field**

- **Definition**: A single unit of data that can be requested in a GraphQL query. Each field is associated with a type and can have arguments and a return type.

Example:

```graphql
type User {
  id: ID!
```

```
  name: String!

  email: String!

}
```

10. **Fragment**

- **Definition**: A reusable portion of a query that can be included in other queries or mutations. Used to avoid code repetition and define common query blocks.

Example:

```graphql
fragment UserFields on User {
  id
  name
}
```

```
query {
  user(id: "1") {
    ...UserFields
  }
}
```

11. **Interface**

- **Definition**: A GraphQL type that defines a set of fields that must be implemented by other types. Used to create polymorphic types that can have different implementations.

Example:

```graphql
interface Animal {
  name: String!
```

```
}


type Dog implements Animal {

  name: String!

  breed: String!

}


type Cat implements Animal {

  name: String!

  livesLeft: Int!

}
```
```

#### 12. **Mutation**

 - **Definition**: A type of operation that allows modifying data on the server. Mutations are used to create, update, or delete data.
```

Example:

```graphql
mutation {
  createUser(name: "Alice", email: "alice@example.com") {
    id
    name
  }
}
```

13. **Query**

- **Definition**: A type of operation that allows reading data from the server. Queries are used to retrieve information without modifying it.

Example:

```graphql
query {
  user(id: "1") {
    name
    email
  }
}
```

14. **Resolver**

- **Definition**: A function that handles requests for a specific field in a query or mutation. Resolvers fetch the data and return it to the client.

Example:

```javascript
```

```
const resolvers = {

  Query: {

    user: (parent, { id }, context) => {

      // Fetch the user from the database

      return getUserById(id);

    },

  },

};
```
```

#### 15. **Schema**

- **Definition**: The definition of the structure of the GraphQL API. The schema defines the types, fields, queries, mutations, and subscriptions available.

**Example:**

```graphql
```
```

```
type Query {

  user(id: ID!): User

}


type User {

  id: ID!

  name: String!

  email: String!

}
```
```

#### 16. **Scalar Type**

- **Definition**: A base type in GraphQL that represents primitive values such as `Int`, `Float`, `String`, `Boolean`, and `ID`. It is not composed of other types.


**Example:**
```

```graphql
type User {
  id: ID!
  age: Int
}
```

17. **Subscription**

- **Definition**: A type of operation that allows clients to receive real-time updates when data changes. Uses WebSocket to maintain an open connection.

Example:

```graphql
subscription {
  userUpdated {
    id
```

```
    name
  }
}
```

18. **Type**

- **Definition**: Represents a data structure in GraphQL. It can be an object type, scalar type, enum type, interface type, or union type.

Example:

```graphql
type Book {
  title: String!
  author: String!
}
```

19. **Union Type**

- **Definition**: A type that can represent one of several different object types. Used to resolve polymorphic types where a field can return multiple different types.

Example:

```graphql
union SearchResult = User | Book

type Query {
  search(query: String!): [SearchResult]
}
```

20. **Variable**

- **Definition**: Dynamic parameters passed to queries and mutations to make requests more flexible. Variables are defined and used within queries to replace hard-coded values.

Example:

```graphql
query getUser($id: ID!) {
  user(id: $id) {
    name
    email
  }
}
```

21. **GraphiQL**

- **Definition**: An interactive user interface for exploring and testing GraphQL APIs. Provides an editor for writing queries and viewing results.

22. **Apollo Client**

- **Definition**: A JavaScript library for state management and interaction with GraphQL APIs. Provides features for caching, query management, and integration with the React framework.

23. **Relay**

- **Definition**: A JavaScript library developed by Facebook for consuming GraphQL APIs. Provides advanced tools for caching, prefetching, and query management in React applications.

24. **Urql**

- **Definition**: A client library for GraphQL with a modular architecture. Provides a set of tools for managing queries and mutations and for integration with React and other libraries.

25. **Apollo Server**

   - **Definition**: A server for GraphQL that implements the GraphQL protocol and provides a reference implementation for building GraphQL APIs with support for advanced features like caching and data management.

26. **GraphQL Yoga**

   - **Definition**: A simple and configurable GraphQL server that provides a default implementation for building GraphQL APIs with support for middleware, subscriptions, and other features.

27. **Apollo Studio**

   - **Definition**: A suite of tools for monitoring, documenting, and managing GraphQL APIs. Offers features for exploring schemas, testing queries, and analyzing performance.

This glossary provides an overview of

essential GraphQL terms and concepts. Understanding these terms is crucial for developing, testing, and maintaining effective and performant GraphQL APIs.

Index

1.Introduction pg.4

2.Fundamental Concepts of GraphQL pg.19

3.Setting Up a GraphQL Server pg.40

4.Writing and Using Queries in GraphQL pg.64

5.Using Subscriptions in GraphQL pg.90

6.Tools and Libraries for GraphQL pg.115

7.Best Practices and Optimization in GraphQL pg.142

8.GraphQL Glossary pg.164